MICHAEL REDHEAD CHAMPAGNE Illustrations **TIFF BARTEL**

WE NEED EVERYONE

HIGHWATER
PRESS

Funded by the Government of Canada
Financé par le gouvernement du Canada

Canadä

Canada Council   Conseil des arts
for the Arts   du Canada

HighWater Press gratefully acknowledges the financial support of
the Government of Canada and Canada Council for the Arts as well as the
Province of Manitoba through the Department of Sport, Culture, Heritage and
Tourism and the Manitoba Book Publishing Tax Credit for our publishing activities.

HighWater Press is an imprint of Portage & Main Press.
Printed and bound in Canada by Friesens
Design by Jennifer Lum
Cover art by Tiff Bartel

Library and Archives Canada Cataloguing in Publication
Title: We need everyone / Michael Redhead Champagne ; illustrations, Tiff Bartel.
Names: Redhead Champagne, Michael, author. | Bartel, Tiff, illustrator.
Identifiers: Canadiana (print) 20220161658 | Canadiana (ebook) 20220161666 | ISBN 9781774920114
(hardcover) | ISBN 9781774920121 (EPUB) | ISBN 9781774920138 (PDF)
Subjects: LCSH: Individuality—Juvenile literature. | LCSH: Ability—Juvenile literature. | LCSH:
Self-realization—Juvenile literature. | LCSH: Helping behavior—Juvenile literature.
Classification: LCC BF723.I56 R43 2024 | DDC j155.2/2—dc23

27 26 25 24   1 2 3 4 5

FSC
www.fsc.org
MIX
Paper from
responsible sources
FSC® C016245

HIGHWATER
PRESS

www.highwaterpress.com
Winnipeg, Manitoba
Treaty 1 Territory and homeland of the Métis Nation

To the North End of Winnipeg,
who raised me to be the person I am today,
and to all the teachers who shine their
light in the darkest places.
—MC

For Charlie.
—TB

Gifts!

Everyone has a gift.

Gifts are skills and talents we share with others. Every gift is different, and every gift is special.

But why do we call it a gift? Because a gift is for sharing with others!

When we practise our gifts, we build ourselves up.
When we share our gifts, we build a strong community.

Our world needs you to share your gift.

What is your gift? Maybe you don't know yet.

Here's how to find your gift in three simple steps:

Step 1 Make a list of three things you like doing.

*I like talking,
I like reading, and
I like doing cartwheels.*

Step 2 Choose one thing on your list that you are good at.

*Even though I like doing cartwheels and reading,
I am best at talking. I love sharing stories (like the
one we're reading), and I can talk all day long.*

Step 3

**Practise and share
your gift!**

*My gift is talking! I love talking to others. I even
practise talking to myself when I write stories!
As a public speaker, storyteller, and helper in my
community, sharing my gift helps me and helps
others too!*

If you still can't think of your gift, ask a friend to help you. They probably see talents in you that you haven't yet realized.

It's okay to ask for help. And it's awesome to help people around you. Helping people might be your gift!

Remember that gifts can come in many forms.

You're an AMAZING friend!

You have the best sense of humour!

You're FUN to be around!

You read SO MANY BOOKS!

Our gifts can help us reach our goals and overcome challenges even when they seem impossible.

When we all work together and use our gifts to solve problems, we can accomplish so much more than we could on our own.

Some people call this activism—I call this building community.
All kinds of gifts are needed to make strong communities.

That's why we need everyone!

We need artists!

Artists bring ideas to life.

You make complicated things beautiful and easier to understand.

You create posters, murals, and more that help everyone get on the same page.

Artists also make amazing creations that everyone sees differently, sparking conversations that can last forever.

We need athletes!

Athletes lead by example and know how to be team members.

You show determination in how you train, how you win, and even how you lose.

You show others how to persevere through low moments and are humble when you win.

Athletes boost morale for communities, countries, or even the whole world!

We need chefs!

Chefs make a difference by sharing a meal with the people they care for!

You help people learn to appreciate different cultures by being adventurous with foods from diverse places.

You can provide food to people who may not have enough to eat.

Chefs and their delicious creations can bring people together in a very special way!

We need gamers!

Gamers strategize and respond to challenges with determination and endurance.

You know how to organize teams and when to take risks.

You imagine new approaches to old problems.

Gamers help us get to the next level and overcome our challenges so we can find success no matter how many times we have to try.

We need storytellers!

Storytellers are libraries on the move!

You write down the stories in your imagination
or capture what's happening in the real world.

Your stories help us learn lessons from the past and inspire good ideas for the future.

Storytellers know there are so many positive things that can happen when we share our stories.

We need good friends!

Good friends help create the greatest memories and offer support when times are tough.

You are a healer and know that laughter is medicine— sharing a smile when someone needs it.

Your friendship helps people understand how special they are.

Good friends build healthy relationships, and healthy relationships build happy communities.

When you share your gift, you give strength to others. Even if you feel too small, too young, or too quiet, your gift is too special to keep to yourself.

If you help your friends find their gifts, then they can help their friends find their gifts, and finding gifts goes on forever! We can put all our gifts together to help our community.

If we all shared our gifts, imagine how much better our world would be. We need everyone to share their gift—especially you!

What is your gift?

Michael Redhead Champagne inspires every time he speaks to an audience or brings his pen to the page. An Ininew public speaker, writer, community advocate, and on-screen personality, his storytelling connects communities across North America and around the world. Michael was born and raised in Winnipeg's North End with family from Shamattawa First Nation. *We Need Everyone* is his first-ever children's book!

Tiff Bartel is an award-winning Viet-Canadian multimedia artist based in Winnipeg. Her body of work includes illustration, filmmaking, design, animation, music, sculpture, and more.

Sushi Meowf is Michael's beloved cat. He loves to play, and his gift is being a good listener.